Teach Me How to Coupon: Couponing 101

KADEN MATTHEWS

Copyright © 2015 Kaden Matthews

All rights reserved.

ISBN: 1516945921
ISBN-13: 978-1516945924

DEDICATION

This book is dedicated to everyone who has watched in amazement as I fed my family with pocket change and asked me to teach them how to coupon.

CONTENTS

CHAPTER 1: INTRODUCTION TO COUPONING

Couponing seems to be the in thing right now. You've seen the extreme couponing shows, you've seen the lady in the supermarket in front of you (holding up the line) with coupons and you've heard about it and now you want in on the action. The problem is, you don't know what to do, much less where to even start.

I'm that lady in front of you at the store with coupons that silently smiles as you and the cashier gawk at my total. You say (and I quote), "I really need to clip some coupons!" or something similar, however, you leave the store and go on with your life until the next time you are standing behind me (or one of my couponing comrades) and remember that you are *still* paying full price.

I'd like you to be a part of my couponing army, so I'm going to give you as much information that I have obtained and successfully used for several years. Hopefully, by the time you are done reading this book, you too will be able to save some coins.

What makes me a coupon expert? I would not necessarily call myself an expert only because it is impossible to know every single thing there is to know about every single coupon and store, and not to mention, the rules are constantly changing. If experience matters though, I have been couponing my entire adult life and I have been "extreme couponing" for several years now.

I have had the extreme stockpile and yes, it's nice to look at, but I have learned that there is a fine line between stockpiling and hoarding. I have a rule now that if the product is not going to be used within a specific period of time or I don't have a place to donate it to immediately, I don't care if the store is paying me $100 to take it off their shelves, I have no use for it and I leave it in the store for someone else to enjoy.

I've abandoned the word "extreme" a while ago, because I am not extreme. Extreme is such an extraordinary word and once I realized the waste that can be associated with it, I've stepped away from it.

There are two different kinds of "extreme" couponers. There is the extreme couponer that has learned to build deals and save every single penny that can possibly be saved on a product, while the other extreme couponer also builds deals and saves quite a bit of money, but they do the deals over and over again, clear shelves and have an excess amount of products that they will most likely never be able to use or give away. If I have to be labeled extreme, then I am the first kind of extreme couponer that I mentioned above. If you want to be the other extreme couponer that I mentioned, it's ok, I won't judge you. Shoot for the moon. I only ask that you find some needy neighbors or charitable organizations to donate your excess products to and not allow them to go to waste.

When people ask me to teach them how to coupon, I chuckle, because I promise you, it is not that difficult. I ask them, "Have you ever used a coupon?" Of course they have, everyone has used a coupon before. If you have used a coupon before, then guess what... You are a couponer!

It really is that simple, cut a coupon and use it.

The end.

Just kidding, I wouldn't do you like that. What they mean to ask me is: "Can you teach me how to coupon, like you?"

I promise, couponing like me is not much more difficult than just plain old couponing.

There is a difference between couponing and "extreme" couponing. Couponing is simple, you clip a coupon and you go purchase a product and save a few pennies on it. Extreme couponing entails maximizing the deal and legally getting every single penny off of a product that you possibly can. Often, you can get the product for free and sometimes, even get paid to purchase the product.

Don't worry, I'm going to show you how to do it and don't

worry, you will be able to do it. You will be a pro in no time at all!

I want you to set realistic expectations, though. While watching people on television get $1200 worth of groceries for $2.98 is exciting, I want you to realize that although it looks good for the television viewing audience, for the most part, it is not how couponing really works.

Most stores put a limit on the number of coupons that can be used. Most stores do not allow multiple transactions. Many cashiers actually look at coupons and confirm that they match the product that you are purchasing and that the coupon is not expired. Stores are notified when there are fraudulent coupons floating around. So everything that you see on television is not necessarily how it really works.

Would you walk in a store and stick a bottle of juice in your purse and walk out? In my opinion, there is no difference between shoplifting and coupon fraud.

I was shocked to learn that people were actually using fake and expired coupons, copying coupons and using coupons for the wrong products and they were actually getting away with it. It is because of these fraudsters, that the stores have had to implement changes. The rules are very clear on coupons, pick one up and read all the small print. Coupon fraud affects all consumers because coupon acceptance changes and prices increase.

So please, don't expect to run out and spend $2.98 on $1200 worth of groceries and then be discouraged when it doesn't happen. Don't misunderstand me, it is legitimately possible, but it is not the everyday norm.

I don't want you to compare yourself to other couponers. I want you to compare your new self to your old self.

Today, look at what you spent on groceries, household, health and beauty products for the past year. Pull out a calculator and add it up. After you begin couponing, I want you to compare those numbers. If you used to spend $700 per month on these products and you are able to cut that down to $500 per month, you are winning.

I'm not saying any of this to discourage you, but I want you to have realistic expectations of what you can do. It is possible to save quite a bit of money when you learn how to do it right.

# CHAPTER 2: GETTING STARTED: FINDING COUPONS

The very most important thing that you need in order to be a couponer is COUPONS!!!

I'm here to tell you, coupons are everywhere. You didn't notice them before because you weren't paying attention. Now that you know, you will be on the lookout and see that they are everywhere.

When I used to "coupon", my only resource for coupons was the Sunday paper. The paper was delivered, I pulled the inserts out, I clipped the coupons that I wanted and put them in an envelope and I threw the rest in the recycling bin. Sometimes I would use the coupons, most of the time, I didn't.

That is why I did not initially understand the "extreme" couponing fad. I didn't understand how they got so many coupons and how they actually saved so much money.

For instance, I would clip a coupon for .20 cents off a can of name brand biscuits. I would get to the store and that can of biscuits would be $2, yet the store brand was only $1. Yes, I could save .20 cents off of the $2 and if I was lucky and at a store that doubled, (I'll explain doubling later) then I could actually get the name brand for $1.60, but, that still didn't make sense to me. I could still get the store brand, which in many instances is just as good as the name brand for $1. This was not winning to me.

So, needless to say, I clipped that .20 cent coupon in vain. I would just go ahead and buy the $1 can of biscuits and throw the

.20 cent coupon in the trash.

If you are just getting started, then you probably think like I used to think, but hopefully, we can work through that.

I don't want to get too far off the topic of *finding coupons* though. I just want to stress now, every coupon that you find is good (unless it's expired). I don't care if it's a product that you have never heard of or think that you won't use. What I am saying is: **Don't clip what you want and throw the rest in the trash.**

Even if you don't immediately find a deal, don't think that you won't be able to find a deal and give up. That is what draws the line between a couponer and a super savvy shopper extraordinaire. Don't worry, I'll get back to this.

Back to finding coupons, like I said before, coupons are everywhere, they are not just in the Sunday paper, although the **Sunday paper** is a wonderful resource for finding coupons. For the most part, you will get coupon inserts in the paper almost every Sunday. There are a few holidays throughout the year that there will be no inserts. You can Google "Sunday Coupon Insert Schedule" at the beginning of each year and you will find several websites that will list the schedule for the year.

The Sunday paper usually has the Red Plum, the Smart Source and the P&G coupon inserts. The Red Plum and the Smart Source usually come out randomly throughout the month and the P&G usually comes at the end of the month and the coupons are usually good for the following month. For instance, the P&G coupon insert may come out Sunday, August 30th and be good for the month of September.

Doesn't the Sunday paper only have one of each coupon in it though? Well that is how you used to think as an ordinary "couponer" but now, you are thinking bigger... Did you know that you can buy more than one newspaper? In fact, some stores actually sell "double papers" at a reduced price or you can always just buy more than one. You can contact your newspaper distributor and pay for multiple sets of papers to be delivered to your home every week.

Some weeks I will buy several papers and some weeks I will only get four. I almost always get at least four papers. I determine the number of Sunday papers that I want to buy by doing a little bit of research. Many websites are available now that will give you previews of the upcoming coupons. Remember though, some coupons are regional, so if you are reading a website that is based out of Georgia and you live in Maine, chances are the coupon may be a different denomination or not even included. The Sunday paper inserts are delivered on Saturday in my area, so I usually look at the inserts that are delivered to my front door and decide if I will buy more from the store on Sunday morning.

I usually purchase my papers from the grocery store because my local store sells double papers so I am able to get two sets of inserts. The grocery store is not the only place that you can buy the Sunday paper though. It is available in drug stores, convenience stores and even dollar stores (although they usually come out on Monday or later at a dollar store). Check around your area and find the best deal for YOU.

Sometimes I will get papers from CVS because I am able to use my ExtraBucks to purchase them. I'll talk about that later though. Just remember, that you are couponing to save money, so it doesn't make sense to spend a fortune to get coupons.

If you decide to have the paper delivered, look for deals online to get it delivered at a reduced rate. Also, don't be afraid to negotiate with the newspaper about your rate. I pay for it for the year and they give me a discount. I also ask my friends and family for their unwanted inserts as they don't have a problem asking for my stockpile. Closed mouths don't get fed.

So, now that you have multiple Sunday papers, let's look elsewhere for coupons, because remember, they are everywhere.

Look for your **free local newspaper**. Sometimes, this paper may be .50 cents give or take, depending on where you live, however, these papers usually have the same inserts that come out on Sunday, just a little less expensive than the Sunday paper. Usually, they even come out a few days in advance. These papers can often be found at your curb (and you've been throwing that newspaper away!), newspaper boxes, the local library, convenience stores, grocery stores, etc. They are there, you just haven't opened them up and discovered that there are coupons inside.

Magazines are also a great source of coupons. Many of the magazines at your local newsstand have coupons inside, you just weren't paying attention. First, check the magazines that are being delivered to your home, there might be some coupons in there. When you are at the newsstand, flip through a few and you will be surprised at what you find. I don't really want to name names (because remember, these folks aren't paying me to drop their names), but I want to make sure that you are getting the most of this. Some of the magazines that I usually try to snag are: All You, Ebony and Good Housekeeping. I have even found free magazines in grocery stores that have recipes and are packed with coupons. Usually the magazines with coupons are geared towards woman, as if men don't want to save money too! Don't be afraid to flip through some other magazines at the newsstand and find some new favorites.

Be on the lookout at grocery stores and drug stores for **coupon booklets**. Coupon booklets can be found just about anywhere in the store, they can be at the customer service desk, a display in the store or even laying on a table somewhere. Just keep an eye out for coupon booklets. Coupon booklets usually have a stack of coupons from the same manufacturer inside. For instance, during back to school time for the past few years, I have been able to find coupon booklets from one particular company that manufactures lunch box treats. The booklet had cookies, chips, fruit cups, etc. I don't mean to get so excited, (but you will too, watch!) but when you find a coupon booklet, sometimes, you have hit the jackpot.

 Coupon booklet

Tearpads and Blinkies are coupons that are found near products and **Peelies and Hangtags** are coupons that are found on products. These coupons can be found in gas stations, grocery stores, drug stores, department stores and convenience stores. Manufacturers distribute these coupons to encourage consumers to purchase their products and it works. If I am in the store and trying to decide on purchasing a product, if I find a coupon attached, I am more likely to purchase that product. If you come across these coupons in the store and you are buying that product, you don't have any excuse not to use the coupon. I've seen people in line at the store with the peelie still attached to their product. Make sense out of that! Who pays full price when they are literally giving it to you?!

 Tearpads

 Blinkies

 Peelies

 Hangtags

Another place to find coupons is on the internet. **Internet Printables** are available all over the internet. Many manufacturers have websites, many of their websites have links to coupons. If you like a particular brand of bread, see if that company has a website and see if they have coupons available on that website. It really is that simple.

Many manufacturers use social media. Go to their social media outlets (Facebook, Instagram, Twitter, etc.) and see if they are offering coupons. There are also websites that are dedicated to internet printable coupons. Some of the websites that I use are: smartsource.com, redplum.com, coupons.com, pillsbury.com, bettycrocker.com, boxtops4education.com and many more. Please note that these websites require that you download their software in order to print coupons from their site. Personally, I have never had any problems with this software, although some are afraid to install it on their computers. This software protects the company against coupon fraud. When you print a specific coupon from one of these sites, you are usually able to print only two copies. Each of these coupons have a unique code that is able to be traced back to your computer. You can't just print a coupon on the internet and go make hundreds of copies of it that is considered fraud.

If you absolutely need more than two, access another computer at your home or job. If you can't use your spouse's or your children's computer, consider purchasing a few inexpensive old used laptops. If you are only using them to print coupons, it's not like you need to spend a lot of money on them.

Do not ever give anyone other than the store one of your internet printable coupons. If you make copies (or if you give one to someone and they make copies), the store does not get paid and the coupons are traced back to your computer and you will no longer be able to print.

Unique code on an internet printable coupon

One great way to get coupons is to **contact the manufacturers directly** and ask for them. That's right! Many manufacturers will send you coupons for their products JUST FOR ASKING. If you like a particular product and you can't seem to find any coupons for it, contact the manufacturer and ask. Look them up on the internet and send them an email. Tell them that you love their product and you would love it so much more if you had a coupon. In no time, your mailbox will be overflowing with coupons. Keep a list of the manufacturers that you contact, how you contacted them and if they sent you anything. If they send something, contact them again in the future (not next week, they will get sick of you) and ask them for more.

If you have read this far, thank you, I am willing to send you over a copy of a list that I use. Contact me on my website at www.kadenmatthews.com and send me your email address and let me know that you are looking for the manufacturer list and I'll send it over to you for free. See look, you haven't even clipped a coupon yet and you are getting stuff for free already, you super savvy saver you!

Another type of coupon is **store coupons**. Yes, there are actually different types of coupons. There are manufacturer coupons (that come from the manufacturer and have manufacturer written at the top) and there are store coupons (that come from the store and have the name of the store imprinted on them – not to be confused with manufacturer coupons that say manufacturer coupon but list a suggested store name). I don't want to confuse you just yet, but often you can stack these coupons together (I'll go over stacking coupons later, I promise). Usually, you can find store coupons throughout the particular store that you are in or in their weekly sale advertisement flyer. These coupons are specific to a particular store. Unless another store accepts competitor's coupons, you won't be able to use these coupons anywhere else.

Target store coupon. Notice the barcode is different from a manufacturer's coupon and it says "Target Coupon".

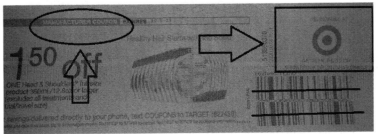

Manufacturer coupon distributed by Target. Notice that it has a manufacturer's coupon barcode and it says "Manufacturer Coupon" across the top. It has a Target symbol on it and says "Redeemable at Target", however, since it is a manufacturer coupon, it should be able to be redeemed at any retailer as long as their coupon policy doesn't forbid accepting coupons with other retailer's logos.

At the beginning of this chapter, I told you: **Don't clip what you want and throw the rest of the coupons in the trash** and I promised you that I would get back to you on this subject.

When I first started couponing, I would go through and only clip the coupons for the products that I used and would throw the rest away. I had no use for them, they were unnecessary clutter.

Once I clipped the coupons and took them to the store and I couldn't find a great deal (for instance, I could get the store brand for cheaper than the name brand product minus the coupon), I would throw the coupon away. This was a big mistake. Learning how to keep and organize coupons and store them until a deal came along made the difference between being an ordinary couponer and an extraordinary couponer.

One thing that I have learned while couponing is that sales always come back around. This week, spaghetti sauce may be $4 a jar, but soon enough it will be on sale for .99 cents. I used to make the mistake of using my coupons right away and not holding on to them for a sale. Generally a coupon is good for about six weeks or so, a sale is bound to come around before that coupon expires. If I need spaghetti sauce right now, I have a coupon for .50 cents, I can go use it on the $4 jar, since I need it right now. But, I will only buy that one jar. I will save the rest of my coupons until a deal comes along and I can stock up. I use spaghetti sauce regularly, so I will stock up when I can get it for .50 cents or less. .50 cents is my **stock-up price**. When I find a deal at my stock-up price, I buy enough product that will last me a few months short of the expiration date. As you begin couponing, you will also determine stock-up prices for products that you regularly use. I hold onto my coupons until a stock-up deal comes along. If it doesn't happen prior to the coupons expiring, then it wasn't meant for me to stock-up on spaghetti sauce this round. But, never fear! Another coupon will come around and there will be a deal on spaghetti sauce and you will be able to get it at your stock-up price soon enough.

I've learned that it pays to save coupons rather than throwing them out whether you plan to use them or not. I may look at the coupon and think that I will never have any use for that product, however, a deal may come up that the product is free or a moneymaker (I'll discuss moneymaker's later) and I might just want to try it then. Also, although I may not want the coupon, one of my coupon friends may have a use for it. I don't cut all these coupons, I leave them in the inserts and I file them in my filing cabinet. I'll talk more about organizing coupons in the next chapter.

I know, I'm turning you into a coupon hoarder, but it's better to be safe than sorry.

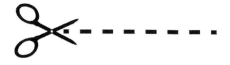

CHAPTER 3: ORGANIZATION

The most important thing that I had to learn and practice is organization. I gave you a lot of resources in chapter 2 where to find coupons, but if you are in the store and can't put your hand on a particular coupon, you've wasted your time.

There are many different common methods of coupon organization and no one particular way is perfect. I will share some of the methods that I have used, but you will eventually learn what works best for you.

When I was just a couponer years ago, I used to put my coupons in a little white envelope or a sandwich bag and keep them in my purse. This particular method does not work well if you have multiple coupons. Occasionally, if I am going into a store now for just a few items or a particular product, I will put the coupons that I plan to use on that trip in an envelope or sandwich bag, but that's not the type of organization that I am talking about here. I am talking about taking your coupon organization to the next level.

The object of coupon organization is to be able to quickly put your hand on a particular coupon for a particular product.

Let's say you are in the store and you come across a deal on some cookies. You know you have that cookie coupon somewhere, is it easier to dig in your purse looking for that coupon or flip open your binder to the snack section and put your hand right on it?

Of course, organization makes sense.

The most common coupon organizer is **the binder**. I know you have seen couponers in the store with their binders flipped across the top of their shopping cart searching for coupons for the products they are buying. You can affordably create your own coupon binder, please don't allow someone to trick you into paying them to make one for you. Remember, you want to coupon to save money, you shouldn't have to spend a fortune to get started. You probably already have many of the supplies to build your own.

Supplies:
3-ring binder: You can find a binder anywhere. You can recycle one of your children's old school binders or you can find a cheap one at a thrift store, a yard sale or an office supply store. Usually during back to school time, you can find a great deal. It doesn't need to be fancy, it is just holding your coupons. I personally prefer one with a zipper because coupons can fall out of the top.

Baseball card holders or currency holders: You can find these at your local office supply store, department store or Amazon and they are not expensive. If you purchase at Amazon, you can share with a friend because you get quite a bit for approximately $10. I use a variety of both the baseball card holder and the currency holders because they hold different size coupons. From here on out, I will refer to these as coupon holders.

Dividers: Available at department stores, office supply stores, or your local dollar store and they are fairly inexpensive, especially during back to school time.

If you have these 3 items, all you need to do is add coupons and you have a coupon binder.

Three-ring notebook binder with coupon holders

TEACH ME HOW TO COUPON: COUPONING 101

Many people also pack a pencil holder in their binder with a calculator (I have one on my phone!) and scissors in case you need to clip a coupon on the run. Also, it is a good idea to carry copies of store policies in your binder as they can sometimes come in handy when an employee does not know their store's policy.

My current coupon binder has a zipper around the side and has accordion files in the front. I have found that this type of binder works best for me. In my accordion files, I keep a few inserts, some loose coupons, rainchecks and store policies.

I chose the names to put on the different tabs of my dividers by what worked for me, you will eventually learn what works for you. My dividers say: Grocery, Dairy, Frozen, Meats, Drinks, Snacks, Pets, Household, Health, Beauty and Miscellaneous. In the past, I have put stickers on the coupon holders breaking them down a little further, for instance under grocery: can goods, bread, etc.

When I clip coupons, I cut them all first, staple them together if I have more than one and then I put them in piles according to the divider that they will be filed under. Then after I am done cutting, I then put them in their slot and I am organized!

Another method of organization that I use is the **filing method**. I've gotten out of the habit of cutting every single coupon that I have and filing them in my binder. It got very time consuming. When I get inserts, I will pull out the coupons out that I am certain that I will use. I file these in my binder. I then file the rest of my inserts in my filing cabinet until I need them. I get multiple inserts each week. I keep one front page of the newspaper (it has the date) and I store the inserts from that week inside the front page of the newspaper. I then file according to date in my filing cabinet.

I rarely go to the store anymore without a plan, so I just don't need to carry all these coupons with me. When I discover a sale, and I need a coupon, I am able to quickly access my filing cabinet and acquire the coupon. When I come across a sale, I search an online coupon database to see if coupons are available. I usually use Couponcadet.com or Southernsavers.com to see if a coupon exists. Both of these particular websites will report if a coupon exists and what week it came out. I am then able to search in my filing cabinet and clip it. Don't forget though, sometimes coupons are regional and they may show up in the online database and not in your local paper or they may have come in your paper and it

21

doesn't show up in their database.

In addition to using the online databases, I also use an app on my android phone called *Coupon Keeper*. I paid $9.99 for this app and it's amazing (to me it is!). You are able to scan the entire insert and log in the app how many copies of that insert that you have. You can search coupons and see if you have them. I'm cheap, I was very apprehensive about giving up $9.99 for the app, but I've been using it now for a while and I love it.

Filing the coupons and searching the databases save me quite a bit of time from cutting coupons that I do not need or will not use. It allows me to save the coupons in case something comes up and I need those coupons.

When I get inserts and I KNOW it is something I will use (for instance I always use that name brand cheese), I will clip those coupons and place them in my binder so I will have them with me at all times.

Accordion binders are another method of coupon organization. They come in different sizes and are available at department stores, office supply stores and dollar stores. I've used both a large and a small accordion in the past. The small one works well if you don't have a lot of coupons and just need a little bit of organization. It conveniently fits in your purse and isn't in the way in the car.

I've used the bigger ones, but it was very disorganized. I used the same tabs like I do on my binder dividers, but didn't have the organization of the coupon holders. Imagine looking in "Grocery" for a bread coupon with no real type of organization. It was a mess. I initially used it because I was tired of filing the coupons in all the individual slots of my coupon holders.

Another method that some people use is an **index card file**. These plastic containers can be found at a dollar store, department store or an office supply store. They usually come with their own little dividers. You can write the different coupon categories across the top.

CHAPTER 4: THE NEXT STEP

So, you've been listening so far and you are ready to coupon. You didn't realize, you were ready to coupon before you even started reading this book. You already have the ability to be a couponer, I hope this this book can transform you into an amazing couponer.

So, if you are really itching to use one of those pretty coupons that you clipped and put in your binder, go ahead and run to the store and use one of those coupons, but come right back so I can help you get to the next level.

So you ran to the store and you bought a jar of mayonnaise for $3.99. You had a .50 cent off manufacturer coupon and the store doubled that coupon, so you saved $1. Congratulations, you are a couponer. But what if I told you that you could have gotten that same jar of mayonnaise for .50 cents?

Remember when I told you back in chapter 1: *Extreme couponing entails maximizing the deal and legally getting every single penny off of that product that you possibly can.*

To get to the next level, the first thing that I would recommend that you do is to **familiarize yourself with the coupon policies** at the stores that you frequently shop at. The policy will state in black and white that store's guidelines on coupons. I have five grocery stores, three drug stores and two major department stores that are in my area that I shop at. When I first started "extreme" couponing, I familiarized myself with the policy at the store that I shopped at the most. I started small and then moved myself up.

You don't have to jump out there and go to every single store and do every single deal, you will burn yourself out and you will have a bunch of junk that you will probably never use in your entire life.

The store coupon policies are available in store, however, they are usually more up to date on their website. I have these store policies printed and I carry them with me in my binder.

Occasionally, you will run across a cashier or a manager that isn't familiar with their store's coupon policy and it doesn't hurt to have it available to show them. One thing that you must understand before arguing with them and making a fool out of yourself, for the most part, the store coupon policies state that the manager has the final say so, so remember, you can catch more bees with honey. You don't want to be *that* couponer that walks in the store and the cashiers and the managers hate you. If you become *that* couponer, you might as well go ahead and throw your binder in the trash because you will never be able to coupon successfully at that store.

Some of the things to look for on these coupon policies is: Do they double coupons? Do they limit the number of coupons that you can double per day? Do they accept competitor's coupons? Do they price match? In a buy one get one free scenario, do they accept a coupon on the free item? Do they limit the number of coupons that you can use? Can you use their online store coupons and manufacturer coupons at the same time? These are just some of the questions that coupon policies answer. Read them. Since I don't shop in every store every day, many times I will have to pull out the store's coupon policy and refresh my memory.

Of the five grocery stores in my area, one store doesn't double coupons at all, I rarely go there unless there is an amazing deal. A few other stores limit the number of coupons that can double. I base my purchases and transactions upon what is allowed in their store. I follow their coupon policies and I rarely have any problems. Occasionally, I will come across an issue, but I am calm and polite and it is usually rectified.

Occasionally you will come upon an un-couponeducated cashier. You are purchasing four similar products and you hand him or her four coupons. They look at the coupons and they say, "You can only use one coupon per purchase." The coupon does state, *one coupon per purchase,* however there is a difference between a purchase and a transaction. You will have to explain to him or her the difference. Your entire shopping trip is a transaction, the one product that you are buying is a purchase. There are some coupons out there that help explain this situation. I keep one of these coupons at the front of my binder to explain it to them in black and white. The coupon says: "Limit of 4 like coupons in the same shopping trip". If you come across one of these coupons, keep it in the front of your binder so you will have it available if you need it. This particular coupon explains it all. If they still try to block you after that, sometimes it is best to either speak with a manager or just leave the products behind.

CONSUMER: LIMIT ONE COUPON PER PURCHASE on any two (2) NIVEA or NIVEA Men Body Wash (8.4 oz. – 25.4 oz.). LIMIT OF 4 LIKE COUPONS in same shopping trip. Coupons not authorized if purchasing products for resale. Void if transferred, sold, auctioned, reproduced or altered from original. Any other

Purchase vs. Transaction

So after you have familiarized yourself with the coupon policies of the stores that you plan to shop at, it's time to begin **building a deal**. To begin building a deal, the next thing that I recommend that you do is to **read the store advertisement flyers**. Read! Read! Read! I can't express this enough, you *must* read these flyers. You can even look at the pretty pictures too. You will not get anywhere if you don't bother reading the store's flyers.

When I read the flyer, I put a star on the items that I may need or may think that it's a great deal. That way, I am able to find them later when I go back through. Of course there is often unadvertised sales and clearance at stores and that is why it pays to carry your coupon binder with you, for the unexpected.

In my area, I have access to five major grocery store chains. I get their flyers regularly. I have learned their sale cycles (some start Wednesday, some start Friday) and I know their coupon policies (you should familiarize yourself with each store's coupon policies that you shop at). I am not loyal to any particular store when it comes to products that I am able to use coupons on. Store A has the same name brand mayonnaise that store B, C, D & E have, so the only thing I care about is the lowest amount of money that I have to spend out of pocket.

At the beginning of this chapter, you paid $2.99 for that jar of mayonnaise while other people without coupons paid $3.99, so realize, you are doing better than the full pricers.

But imagine this: that jar of mayonnaise was $3.99 at store A, but had you checked your weekly flyers, you would have seen that it is on sale at store C this week for $2.50. Yes, you can use coupons on sale items! Store C also doubles coupons, just like store A, so your .50 cent coupon would still double to $1, so without any other steps, you will have gotten that same jar of mayonnaise for $1.50. BUT!!! There are other steps (levels folks!). In that same flyer for store C, there is a store coupon for .50 cents off the mayonnaise. You are able to stack the .50 cent manufacturer coupon that doubled to $1 with the .50 cent store C coupon to save a total of $1.50, bringing the jar of mayonnaise down to $1. BUT WAIT!!! There's more!

There are some apps that give you money back to shop. A few of the apps that I use are **SavingStar, Ibotta** and **Checkout51** (look up these apps on your phone and add them and register your store savings cards). There are other apps, but I will go over apps later. Some apps use your store loyalty card and others require that you upload your receipt after you purchase a product. Anyways, one of these apps is giving you .50 cents in the form of a rebate if you purchase that particular jar of mayonnaise. So your $1 that you paid for the mayonnaise has turned into .50 cents.

Meanwhile, the full pricers are at store A paying $3.99.

This is why I say READ YOUR STORE ADVERTISEMENT FLYERS!!!

So, you've familiarized yourself with their coupon policy and you've read their advertisements and you found a few items that you may want or need.

The first thing I do is I go to one of the coupon databases that I mentioned back in chapter 3 to see if there are coupons available and if I have them. (Remember: I use Couponcadet.com and Southernsavers.com and the Coupon Keeper app).

If I have the coupons, I pull the insert and I clip the coupons.

I then look to see if I can find anything else. I look in my apps (SavingStar, Ibotta and Checkout51) to see if there is a deal, I check the flyers to see if there are any store coupons. I check online to see if there are any Catalina deals.

What is a **Catalina**? A Catalina is the coupon that prints out of the little machine on the side of the cash register. Sometimes, there are deals that if you purchase a specific amount of a product, you will get a Catalina to use on your next order. For instance, the mayonnaise could have had a deal that if you buy 4 you will get a coupon to save $2 on your next order. In the deal that I mentioned above where you paid .50 cents for your mayonnaise, if you had purchased 4, you would have gotten a $2 on your next order (O.N.Y.O.) Catalina back, making that .50 cent mayonnaise, free.

There used to be a specific website that I liked that listed all of the Catalina deals but the site is no longer available. Now, I usually just Google Catalina deals and see what's out there. Also, pay attention to the Catalinas that you get from the register because they often advertise upcoming Catalina deals.

When you get the $2 Catalina back from purchasing the mayonnaise, you are able to use that on *anything* in your next order. You can go buy a twelve pack of cola and get $2 off the cola. It is your "store money" to spend on anything that you want.

This really is what "extreme" couponing is about. You familiarize yourself with the stores and then you use all the resources that you have available to you to build a deal and maximize absolutely everything that you can legitimately save off of a product.

I promise that it isn't as hard as it seems, in time, it will soon become second nature.

CHAPTER 5: REPROGRAMMING

You have been shopping your entire life. You are set in your ways. It is time to change some of the information that has been embedded in your mind.

We have been taught to buy in bulk. More is better. We have warehouse clubs that claim to be the best deal. Unfortunately, some of those warehouse clubs, in additional to charging a fee to step in the front door, don't even allow you to use coupons. I don't know about you, but every time I have ever gone into one of those stores I have always spent much more than I would have spent at the grocery store.

While the cost per ounce is usually less on a bigger package of a product, when you are able to use coupons, the final out of pocket on a smaller package is usually less expensive.

For instance, a box of cereal may cost $3 for 20 ounces but $5 for 40 ounces. The $3 box is .15 cents per ounce while the $5 box is 12.5 cents per ounce. If you aren't using coupons, of course the bigger box makes more sense, you are only paying 12.5 cents per ounce rather than .15 cents per ounce.

Let's pretend that you have a coupon for $1.25 off one box of cereal and the size requirement is 20 ounces or more. You will be able to get the 20 ounce box for $1.75 or the 40 ounce box for $3.75 after the coupon. After the coupon, the 20 ounce box becomes .0875 cents per ounce while the 40 ounce box becomes .09375 cents per ounce. After coupons, the 20 ounce box is less expensive.

It is usually best to get the smallest product allowed per the specifications of the coupon.

One of my bad habits that I had to break was laziness. I always went to the grocery store that was closest to my home for convenience. I didn't care if the item was on sale or not, I just wanted to get in and out. I hated spending time in the grocery store anyways, so having to go to a different store just to save a few dollars seemed crazy to me. I was loyal to the store near my home because I did like their quality, however, the same exact brand of mayonnaise is exactly the same whether I am getting it from store A, B, C, D or E. I had to reprogram myself to go to the store with the lowest prices even if it was a little bit out of my way. Eventually, I learned that the more I stocked up on items that I regularly used, the less that I would need to go to the store in the future.

Don't get fooled by marketing tactics at the grocery store. What may seem like a deal is not necessarily a deal. It is wise to keep a notebook of prices that you usually pay for a product. You will see how they mark the price of products up in order to put them on sale. They will try to trick you with the 10 for $10 deals (you don't need to buy 10 products to get that price). Grocery stores have marketing geniuses who work extremely hard to get all of your money. They often put the more expensive products at eye level so you have to look for the less expensive products. They put products on the end caps so you will subconsciously think that they are on sale. You have to outthink these folks.

In your notebook of prices, also keep a running list of your best prices. I keep stock-up prices in my notebook. There are just some items that I refuse to pay over a certain amount of money for. For instance, I have always been able to work a deal and get shampoo and toothpaste for free. I just don't feel comfortable paying for these items anymore. There are other items that I feel should cost just pennies before I start throwing it in my shopping cart. I don't feel comfortable paying more than .20 cents for pasta or .50 cents for pasta sauce. I can't fathom paying more than a dollar for a case of water. Dog treats should be free.

I could go on for days about the items that I refuse to pay for, but I don't want to overwhelm you right now. Just know that there will come a time in your life when you too will be too good to pay for toothpaste.

Another bad habit that I had to get out of was being brand loyal. Don't get me wrong, in my mind there is only one type of mayonnaise and one type of bread that I will eat. If I come across a deal for another brand, I won't turn my nose up at it, I will get it for another family member. In the past though, I was so brand loyal that I refused to try anything new. Coupons and getting free products helped me get over that loyalty real quick. I ventured out and I tried new products and eventually learned that many of them are the same. The only difference is free and cheap tastes a lot better.

It's easy to get excited when you finally crack the code and are able to get some products for real cheap or free. It is exhilarating. I remember my first "haul" of free products was fruit snacks. I think I got a lifetime supply. I was so excited about getting free fruit snacks that I didn't even consider that no one in my family really likes them. I just thought FREE! I had to have them. That was the first and last time that I went crazy. I gave the majority of those boxes of fruit snacks away and since then, anytime I come across an amazing deal, I ask myself if my family really needs this product. If I have to think about it, the answer is no. I don't waste my time nor my energy. But it's free you say, it's a moneymaker, you say... honestly, my time and energy is worth more than both if there is no use for the product in my home. Now, before I buy anything, it must have a place to go to. If it's not in my home then it must go to its destination on my way home. I had to teach myself that free isn't always free.

Once you begin couponing, you will begin to learn the shelf life of products. While it is wonderful to have a stockpile of free toothpaste or spaghetti sauce, if it goes bad before you can use it, you wasted your time and energy collecting it. Therefore, learning shelf life is important. Always remember to check expiration dates when you purchase an item and when you store it on your shelf, put the newest purchases at the back. I use FIFO (First In, First Out) canned food organizers and use the same method with all of the products that I purchase. With FIFO organization, you will use the items in the order that you purchased them to help avoid expiration and waste.

In my opinion, you can never go wrong with a stockpile of toilet paper, paper towels, feminine products, paper plates, plastic cups, trash bags and a few other non-perishables. Any time I come across an amazing non-perishable deal, I try to get as much as I possibly can. I am always trying to build deals for these products.

If you discover that possibly, you have purchased too much, don't be afraid to donate it. In addition to friends and family who would love your overstock, don't forget about your elderly neighbors, especially those on a fixed income. The shelters and pantries also have the need for free products. Often, your donation to charitable organizations can be tax deductible.

CHAPTER 6: STORE LOYALTY

Most of the stores in my area have store customer loyalty cards. If you don't have a customer loyalty card and consistently use it, then you are missing out on a lot of deals.

None of the stores in my area charge to have their loyalty card, so I am assuming that they should be free everywhere. It is as simple as going to the customer service desk and asking for one.

Most stores have sales that are only available to those customers who have the loyalty card. The full price shopper can still shop at the store, but they will pay regular price. When you scan your loyalty card at the register, money will come off.

The loyalty cards also make it simple for the stores to market you with products that you usually purchase. Often, I get coupons in the mail from the stores that I have loyalty cards from.

Additionally, many of these stores link the loyalty cards to an online website where you are able to go online and add additional coupons to your customer loyalty card.

So say for instance, the shelf price is $3 for a loaf of bread, however if you use your loyalty card, you get the sale price, so the same bread is $2. If you go to the online website or the store app, you may be able to also load a .50 cent coupon for the same bread onto your card. When you go to the register, the bread will ring up for $3, but when you scan your card, you will get the sale price of $2 and then the coupon that you loaded onto your card of .50 cents will also come off, making that $3 loaf of bread only $1.50. If you have a manufacturer's coupon, you should also be able to use that coupon with this deal taking even more money off.

Depending upon your store, some loyalty cards will accumulate points for different programs. A few of the stores in my area accumulate gas points on the loyalty cards. I am able to take my loyalty card to the local gas station and save money off at the gas pump.

So don't bypass the store loyalty cards. Don't just ask the cashier if you can use hers. Go get your own. Stop leaving money on the table and stop giving her all of your gas points.

CHAPTER 7: CASH BACK APPS

In the chapter 4, I mentioned cash back or rebate apps. I want to explain a few of these apps so you can understand their value and their importance to your couponing game.

After you have studied your store flyer and found coupons to match up with a sale and have utilized all deals on your store loyalty card and even gotten back a Catalina or two and you thought that you have saved absolutely all the money that you thought was possible to save, who would have thought that there is even more money to be had?

After all the deals are done, in the store, there are cash back or rebate apps that will get you even more money off and lower your total out of pocket.

Most of the apps that I use are available on both Apple and Android systems. I'm sure that there are other apps out there, but the apps that I am going to tell you about, I use personally and have gotten quite a bit of money back from them.

SavingStar is an app that you can add on your phone. In the application, you will add your store loyalty cards, like your local grocery store, CVS, Walgreens, etc. The program tracks the purchases that you make while using your store loyalty card. You do have to go into the application and select current deals in order to get them. It's very simple, you open up the app, click on the product (I click them all) and add them to your card. I go in once a week, usually on Friday, and update all the deals. I choose Friday, because there is usually a Friday deal every week. If you do not add the product, you will not get the rebate.

The deals that you find listed may be something like .50 cents off a particular brand of chips. When you purchase that particular item in the store, your loyalty card will register that you purchased the bag of chips and the rebate money will be transferred to your SavingStar account. The money takes about a week or so to be added to your account after you purchased it (although it varies from store to store). After you accumulate enough money, you are able to then transfer that money to your PayPal account.

SavingStar is free money for items that you are already purchasing.

Another app that I use is **Ibotta**. If you aren't using Ibotta yet, go download the app and please use my referral code: 6b6ta. I get bonus credit when I share the application with others (and you will too after you share). Often, many of the deals that are on SavingStar are also on Ibotta so you are able to get double rebates, also many of these items even have current coupons available, you are able to use both the manufacturer coupon, the store coupon if there are any and the rebate app. In Ibotta, you are able to browse the different stores that you shop at and choose an item that you purchased. In the store, you can use the barcode scanner to confirm that the item is the correct size, flavor, etc. Then after you have purchased it, you take a picture of your receipt and scan the barcode of the product and you are notified that there is a match and you get the rebate reward deposited into your account. You must have $5 in your account to cash out. You can cash out to a PayPal account. The various products can get you anywhere from .25 cents to a few dollars back. Again, just like SavingStar, it is just extra bonus money on products that you are already buying.

Currently, they have team bonuses on Ibotta. When you connect to Facebook, your Facebook friends become your team. When the members of your team redeem rebates within a specific period of time, everyone in the team who participates gets a cash bonus. Additionally, almost all the time they have something that is a non-brand specific staple that will get you some money back, for instance: milk, bread, eggs or vegetables.

Another free app that I use is **Checkout51**. In my opinion, Checkout51 is a just a smaller version of Ibotta. There is a limited amount of deals that you can cash out on, however they usually have something that we are more likely to purchase. If we are going to purchase it anyways, we might as well get some extra money back. For instance, they have yogurt, bananas and tomatoes this week (amongst other items). You have to select the item that you have purchased and take a picture of your receipt and then upload it. They review your receipt and confirm that the product was purchased and then the money goes into your account. You must have a balance of $20 to cashout to a PayPal account. It is not hard to get to $20. I have cashed out a few times.

Another app that I don't use as often as I should is **Receipt Hog**. I just keep forgetting to upload my receipts! It's very simple and easy to make money on Receipt Hog though, if you do it. No matter what you buy at the store, you get credit for uploading your receipts. It's that simple, you take a picture of the receipt with your smart phone and upload it to Receipt Hog and you get points for your receipt. After you gain 600 coins, you can cash out for $5.

If you haven't signed up for Receipt Hog yet, please use my referral link so we can both get free spins to get free coins or even win the amount of our last shopping trip! The link to use is: http://app.receipthog.com/share/aim7s883

There are many other apps available to get cash back, you just have to explore your phone and the internet to find them. I just mention these apps because I have personally used them and I have personally received cash from them so although I do not work for the company, nor am I being compensated in any way, shape or form to endorse them, from my personal previous experience, they are legitimate.

I use a few other apps that are not cash back apps but help me in my shopping adventures. The Amazon app allows me to search items while in the store to make sure that I am getting the best price possible. If I'm at a store (like Walmart) that price matches Amazon, and you find it cheaper on Amazon, you can get Walmart to price match.

The Target Cartwheel App allows you to scan a product while in the store and see if there is a Cartwheel deal to add to your card to save even more money.

CHAPTER 8: DOUBLING COUPONS

In chapter 4, I touched on couponing policies and building deals. I want to further explain what some of this stuff means so you can better understand.

Doubling coupons: In my area, we are very fortunate that many of our grocery stores double coupons. Usually, department stores and drug stores do not double coupons, only grocery stores. You will need to check your store's coupon policy to see if they "double" coupons.

Generally stores that double coupons will double a coupon under .99 cents. What that means is:

If you have a coupon that is .99 cents off a product, that coupon will double to $1.98. If you have a .75 cents off coupon, it will double to $1.50. Sometimes a coupon will state "do not double", that however does not mean that a coupon will not double when it is scanned. For the most part, you can look at a coupon and you will be able to tell if that coupon will double or not.

When you look at the bar code of a coupon, there are a lot of numbers.

UPC coupon barcode

37

This is an UPC coupon. This is the older, more common bar code used on a coupon. The first set of numbers is the number system character. This number is usually a 5 or a 9. This is the number that you can look at and determine if a coupon will double or not. Usually, if this number is a 5, the coupon will double at stores that double coupons and if it is a 9, it will not. The number system character tells the computer that it is scanning a coupon and not a product.

If the barcode starts with a 5, usually it will double:

If the barcode starts with a 9, usually it will not double:

The second set of numbers is the manufacturer code, on the UPC coupon on the previous page, it is 04142. The manufacturer code refers to the manufacturer of that product. If you look on a UPC code on a product, these five numbers should match the first five numbers of that product.

The next three digits, in this case 110, is the product code, on this coupon. The product code matches the particular product under that manufacturer.

The next two digits, in this case 72, is the value code. The value code represents the value of the coupon. This particular coupon was worth $6, so 72=$6 off the product. See the diagram on the next page for some common coupon values.

Code	Value	Code	Value
00	Free	74	$5
07	$1.50/3	75	.75
08	$3/2	76	$1
09	$2/3	77	$1.25
13	$1/4	78	$1.50
14	Buy 1 Get 1 Free	80	.80
16	Buy 2 Get 1 Free	81	$1.75
25	.25	82	$2
33	$1/2	83	$2.25
36	$1.50/2	84	$2.50
42	$1/3	85	.85
50	.50	86	$2.75
51	$2/2	87	$3
55	.55	90	.90
60	.60	91	$3.50
61	$10	95	.95
65	.65	99	.99
70	.70	00	Intervention

Coupon Value Codes are the last two numbers in the third set of numbers on a UPC coupon. These two numbers determine what the value of the coupon is. As always, with anything when it comes to couponing, this is subject to change and is only a list of the more popular denominations.

The final number on the UPC coupon, in this case 1, is the check digit. The check digit is used by the computer to make sure that the bar code is correctly composed.

Manufacturers began using new, more advanced barcode coupons in the mid-80s, however UPC coupons still remain the most common coupon barcode used in the United States. GS-1 barcodes are more difficult for the consumer to read and determine if the coupon will double. There are some apps that you can scan these coupons to check if they will double. GS-1 coupons were implemented to allow for more information such as size and expiration date to be coded into the coupon code.

GS-1 coupon barcode

CHAPTER 9: STACKING

If you've done any research on couponing, I'm sure you've come across the term **stacking** before. This is one way that couponers save a lot of money.

When you use a coupon, remember, you may only use ONE manufacturer's coupon on ONE product. Remember, manufacturer's coupons are distributed by the manufacturer to promote sales of their product by offering money off. You cannot use more than one manufacturer coupon per product. You can't use two manufacturer coupons on one product, it doesn't work that way, otherwise why not use ten and get it for free? If a coupon is for two products (for instance save $1/2 cans of soup), then you can only use one coupon for two products as defined in the terms of the coupon.

Remember, I told you about **store coupons** back in chapter 2. Stores will sometimes distribute coupons to save money off the products in their stores. The store coupon is only supposed to be used in that particular store. You should be able to look at a coupon and tell the difference between the two. If you can't now, don't worry, you will be able to soon. A manufacturer's coupon says "Manufacturer's Coupon" across the top and has a barcode that looks like the coupons mentioned previously. A store coupon will not have manufacturer's coupon written on it. It may say the store name on it and will have a different type of barcode. Don't be confused though, some coupons will have a store name on the coupon, however, they will say "Manufacturer's Coupon" across the top. These are manufacturer's coupons and the manufacturer is just suggesting that you use the coupon at that particular store because that store has most likely paid to advertise on that coupon. Some stores will allow you to use this coupon even if it has another store listed on the coupon and some stores will not. It depends on the store's coupon policy. Go back to chapter 2 and review the pictures of the two different "Target" coupons. Those graphics will help you understand the difference between store and manufacturer coupons.

Back to the point. If you have a manufacturer's coupon and a store coupon for the same product, and the store allows stacking, you will be able to use two coupons on the same product. Example: You have $1 off 1 jar of mayonnaise manufacturer coupon and you have .50 cents off 1 jar of mayonnaise store coupon, you are able to use BOTH of these coupons together and save $1.50 off that one jar of mayonnaise.

CHAPTER 10: COUPON TRADE

Before I started couponing, I had no idea that there were other coupons than the ones that landed on my front doorstep when the newspaper delivery man dropped the paper off on Sunday morning. Honestly, I never thought about it.

Did you know that coupons differ in different areas? For instance, in my area, it is very common for stores to double coupons up to .99 cents, but in some areas in the United States, it is unheard of. So it is common for my area to get a coupon for $1 that will not double, but another area (that doesn't double) to get a coupon for .75 cents for the same product. That coupon would double in my area, taking $1.50 off a product, but it wasn't distributed here. It sometimes seems like the manufacturer wants to block us from saving more money by controlling what coupons we get in our area.

Also, my area may not get a specific coupon that was distributed in another part of the country. It's frustrating if it is a coupon that you need to complete a deal.

Manufacturers strategically place their coupons in different markets to utilize the most of their budget.

Please note that coupons do state that they are void if transferred, sold, etc. However, many people do trade coupons with their friends.

Usually, I will purchase twenty copies of a newspaper and in those inserts, I will have twenty baby powder coupons. I do not have a baby and I do not use baby powder, but if I have a friend that has a baby and will use the coupons that I paid for when I purchased the newspapers, then I see nothing wrong with giving her something that I would have otherwise thrown away.

CHAPTER 11: GETTING THE MOST OUT OF THE GROCERY STORE... (PUTTING ALL THAT YOU'VE LEARNED IN ACTION)

I am going to walk you through getting the most out of a few stores. Over the next few chapters, I will discuss a grocery store, a drug store and a department store. Even if you do not have these particular stores in your area, understand that a lot of this information is universal. I obviously cannot know about every single store in the United States nor know how to shop there, but if I moved to a different area, I would be successfully shopping in no time. I want you to be able to take the information that I give you and make it work at your store.

The best way to start couponing is to jump right in. My advice would be to start at the store that you have been shopping at without coupons until you learn the ropes and then you can venture out.

Before I became an amazing couponer, I used to buy all my groceries at **Safeway** and I used to buy all of my household, health and beauty products from Walmart. Safeway/Vons is available in a few states across the United States, however their policies slightly differ in the various states and Walmart obviously is everywhere.

Although I still shop at Safeway often (because they have some great deals), I rarely go to Walmart anymore because although their prices are slightly lower, they do not double coupons. I can use a coupon at a store that doubles and I am able to get the product for less than if I got it at Walmart.

Back to the point, the best place to start couponing is to shop where you know. What do you know about your "favorite" store? Do you know their coupon policy? Do they even accept coupons? Start by either visiting their website or Googling their coupon policy.

Go read their coupon policy directly from their website.

What you are looking for in a coupon policy is:

- Do they take coupons?
- Do they double coupons? How much do they double to?
- Do they take competitor's coupons?
- Do they price match their competitors?
- How many coupons can you use in a transaction?
- Do they have store coupons and do they allow you to stack store coupons with manufacturer coupons?
- Do they accept internet printable coupons? Some stores no longer accept IP coupons because people have abused these. You cannot make copies of coupons. That is coupon fraud.
- Does the store give rainchecks?

Of course, other information will be provided, but the best thing to do is to print and read your current favorite store's coupon policy to familiarize yourself with it.

When I used to shop at Safeway, I knew that they had a loyalty program, however, I did not have my own card. I used to use my mother's phone number. Once I began couponing, I got my own card.

At Safeway, you are able to get the "Club Price" when you have the Safeway Club card, without the card, you will pay full price.

After you obtain your Safeway Club Card, you have to go online and register for their Just4U website and add the Just4U app to your phone. You can either use the website or your phone, whichever is more convenient for you. There is nothing extra on either the app or the website.

Just4U has coupon deals that all members have access to and personalized deals that are personalized to you. The personalized deals are based upon your previous purchases. Very often, I will get free products on my Just4U app, I just need to add them to my card, find the product in the store and check out.

Many times, I will sit in the car before walking in the grocery store and add items to my card right from my phone.

Be sure when you add the items to your phone that you check how often you can use that same deal. Sometimes, it will be unlimited and other times it will be a one-time use.

Please, if you aren't understanding just how easy this is, visit the customer service desk and ask the manager to show you.

So after you've familiarized yourself with their coupon policy and added your loyalty card to the Just4U website/app, the next thing to do is to familiarize yourself with the store. Safeway sales run from Wednesday morning until Tuesday night. Sometimes, they have sales that are either Friday only or 3-day only (the weekend). Sometimes their sales will last longer, you just need to read the yellow tag in the store (it will say thru Tue. Nov 02, etc. at the bottom).

When I get their flyer, I look for the products that I usually purchase and then I look for coupons on the coupon databases (Couponcadet.com and Southernsavers.com) to match the sales. I check Just4U to see if there is any other deals to be had and I check my rebate apps (SavingStar, Ibotta and Checkout51) to see if I need to add the product.

Although this example was Safeway, your local grocery store is probably similar. Visit their website or ask at the customer service desk.

CHAPTER 12: GETTING THE MOST OUT OF THE DRUG STORE... (PUTTING ALL THAT YOU'VE LEARNED IN ACTION)

After I mastered saving money at Safeway, I moved onto **CVS**. Prior to couponing, I used to get all of my household, health and beauty products from Walmart, but now CVS is one of my most favorite places to shop and use coupons now.

The best thing that I can recommend is to jump right in and start using coupons and you will be swimming in no time.

First review CVS' current coupon policy. You can either find it on their website or Google it. Remember coupon policies do change often and ultimately, the final decision is on the manager. CVS is a small store and if you are shopping their frequently, they will become familiar with you. It is important to build a strong, positive relationship with the cashiers and managers. If you learn how to coupon correctly and legitimately, these employees will realize that you aren't there to get over on them, you are there to save a few dollars legitimately and you will be able to build a strong, trusting relationship.

As of the last time that I read the CVS policy, this is CVS' coupon policy in a nutshell: CVS allows 1 manufacturer coupon and 1 CVS coupon per product. You can use multiple dollar off coupons in one transaction as long as they apply (for instance if you have 2 $3/15 coupons and you are purchasing over $30 in this transaction, you can use 2 of the coupons). In addition to these discounts, you can also use unlimited ExtraBuck rewards as they are applied as cash.

In my opinion, the best part of CVS' coupon policy is their **buy 1 get 1 free promotions** combined with buy 1 get 1 free coupons. For instance, if CVS has a promotion going on of buy 1 get 1 free laundry detergent and at the time there is a coupon out for buy 1 get 1 free laundry detergent, you are able to use the b1g1 free coupon on the b1g1 free sale promotion and you will be able to get both products for free. Yes, free. Also, if there is a buy 1 get 1 free promotion and you have a $1 off coupon, you are able to use two $1 off coupons, as CVS allows you to use a coupon on both products, even in a buy 1 get 1 free scenario. So if they have a b1g1 free promotion on laundry detergent and they are on sale for $6 buy 1 get 1 free, without any coupons, they are technically $3 each. If you have $1/1 laundry detergent coupons, you would then be able to use 2 - $1 coupons on the two products bringing their price down to $2 each.

Please note that you cannot use a b1g1 free *manufacturer coupon* and a dollar off *manufacturer coupon* on the same set of products. A b1g1 free coupon is attached to two products. You cannot then use a $1 off manufacturer coupon on the "free" product. Coupons read – 1 coupon per purchase. A purchase is one product. You cannot use 2 manufacturer coupons on 1 product. If you have a store coupon and a manufacturer coupon, then you would be ok.

Some people will try to tell you otherwise and even if the "store" allows it, it is not the right way to coupon. It is not up to the store to allow it, as the manufacturer who distributes the coupon says otherwise. The manufacturer is the one who is paying the store back for accepting the coupon. Remember, the coupon reads – 1 coupon per purchase.

Things that you need to know about CVS: You need a CVS extra care card. These are available at the front register. Most of CVS' sales require that you use the CVS extra care card. Once you get the extra care card, be sure to link your telephone number to the card, that way if you lose your card (or you are just too lazy to take it out of your purse like me), you will be able to give the cashier your phone number to still receive the sale price. Don't forget to provide CVS with your email address. I get emails from CVS several times a month with amazing coupons, like $3 off any $15 purchase, etc. These coupons are good on anything in the store and can be stacked with manufacturer and store coupons.

You will also need to know about the **Red Box**. When people speak about CVS, you will often hear them mention the Red Box. The Red Box is not the box out front that you are able to rent movies from, it is the red machine usually towards the front of the store that is red and has CVS Extra Care Coupon Center written on it.

The CVS Extra Care Coupon Center "Red Box" is often located at the front of CVS near the registers. It doubles as a price checker and store coupon machine. I always use the price checker at CVS especially on clearance items. Often, the yellow clearance tag will say that the item is on clearance for 25%, however, they have not gotten around to updating the tag and it is really discounted to 75% now. I *always* double check clearance items. Don't forget, you can use coupons on sale and clearance items.

You should scan your Extra Care Card upon entering the store and always scan it until it tells you that there are no more coupons. The Red Box disperses various CVS "Extra Care" coupons. These coupons can be used in addition to manufacturer coupons. In other words, you can "stack" these coupons with manufacturer coupons to get extra savings on a product.

In this particular scenario above, I have received a $3/$10 purchase of (ANY) Razors, Blades or Shave creams/gel. I check to see if I have any Razor coupons and I have a Buy 1 Gillette Male Razor, get 1 Free Gillette Shave Prep (up to $6) free. So, I can purchase a razor and a shave gel as long as it totals up to $10 or more and I can save $3 from the CVS extra care coupon and up to $6 on the shave gel from the manufacturer coupon. For example, I find a $7 razor and a $6 container of shave gel, my total comes to

$13. I am able to save a total of $9 (the $3 CVS coupon and the $6 manufacturer coupon), my total out of pocket for both the razor and the shave gel is $4.

Let me say this one more time, so you can hear me: SCAN YOUR EXTRA CARE CARD MORE THAN ONCE! Often there are more coupons that come out. You won't get duplicate coupons, but very often you get more. When you can't scan anymore, the screen will tell you, "hey Super Scanner, you've gotten all your coupons today…" Also, note the expiration date on your ExtraBuck coupons, for the most part they won't expire this week. Often these dates are well into the next few weeks. I save my extra care coupons for the sale that may happen in the near future.

Please note that the last 4 digits on the extra care coupon and extra care rewards match the last 4 digits of your reward card. Although many people leave the coupons that they do not want at the red box coupon center, these coupons are worthless to you. The coupons and rewards match your card.

In addition to the manufacturer coupon savings and the Extra Care coupon savings, CVS may be having a promotion for these items that could result in an **ExtraBuck Reward**. An ExtraBuck reward (often referred to as ExtraBucks, EBs, or even ECBs – as they used to be called extra care bucks) are different from an extra care coupon. An ExtraBuck is earned on the purchase of a particular product and can be used just like cash inside of CVS.

In this particular promotion, CVS says spend $25 on select Gillette cartridges, razors, shave gels, select Secret or Old Spice deodorant. If you used the coupons above, you could get 2 razors and 2 free shave preps (as long as they come up to $25 BEFORE coupons). You would be able to use 1 $3/$10 EB Coupon and 2 of the b1g1 free manufacturer coupons. Remember I found the $7 razor and the $6 shaving gel, one set would come to $13, so if I get two sets, I'd be at $26. I would save $3 off the total bringing me to $23 and then use two of the manufacturer coupons and save another $12, bringing me down to $11 out of pocket. After I spend $11 out of pocket, I would get a $5 ExtraBuck reward to use on my next shopping trip. This would make the total out of pocket for this trip only $6. The idea is to use ExtraBuck rewards on purchases that result in more ExtraBuck rewards (this is often referred to as **flipping EBs**).

This deal: $7 razors x 2 = $14. 2 Shave preps $6 x 2 = $12.

$14+$12=$26-$12 (free shave prep) = $14 - $3 (ExtraBuck coupon) = $11 - $5 (the ExtraBuck reward) = $6

Flipping or Rolling ECBs: So the next time I come to CVS, I have $5 in ECBs to spend from this deal. I can spend that $5 on anything in the store (usually not gift cards, tobacco products or prescriptions). I usually try to find something that I can invest that $5 in and take another $5 out. For instance, had I started out the last scenario (with the razors) with $5 in ECBs, instead of spending $11 in cash and getting a $5 ECB reward, I would have spent $6 in cash and a $5 ECB reward and got back $5. My total out of pocket would have been $1 instead if I count the reward as cash back. $11 is the - $5 ECB = $6 (paid in cash) receive a $5 ECB back to use the next time = total out of pocket $1.

I know it sounds confusing, but once you try it and get the hang of it, it will become easy. I am able to stand in the middle of the store and work these math problems out in my head.

By the way, even if you are only paying $3 out of pocket on $35 worth of merchandise, you will still have to pay taxes on $35 worth of product. Uncle Sam has to get his.

One thing that I like to buy with my CVS ExtraBucks is the Sunday paper. Why pay cash for it if you have extra CVS cash that can cover it?

CVS Discount Order:

It has been my best experience to present my discounts in this order:

1. Extra Care Card
2. CVS ExtraBuck Rewards
3. CVS Extra Care Coupons
4. Manufacturer Coupons

If they insist that you do it another way, it is ultimately up to the store the order that they want to take your coupons in. But in this discount order scenario, they are able to mark down a manufacturer's coupon. I've been told that they can't mark down the extra care coupons, although I have seen it done. Remember, marking down a coupon occurs when overage is going to occur. CVS does not give overage.

Remember to get a raincheck

Unfortunately, when there is a great sale, often the shelves are clear. Get a raincheck. A CVS raincheck will allow you to come back to the store and get the sale price of that item when they come back in stock. They will also write the promotion on the raincheck so if there are ECB rewards attached, you can get those later too. Personally, I love when I have a raincheck and a better coupon comes along. Most stores will give a raincheck when they are out of a product although their policies may vary. For instance, one grocery store in my area gives rainchecks that are good for 90 days after the end of the sale, while another has no expiration date on their rainchecks. Rainchecks are very valuable little pieces of paper. If you go to the store and the product is not available, it is the very least that the store can do to compensate you for your time.

Sign up for the CVS Beauty Club

If you spend $50 on beauty products while using your Extra Care card you will earn a $5 ExtraBuck reward. You can earn this reward as many times as you hit $50. The bottom of your receipt will say how much more that you have to spend in order to get this award. This calculates BEFORE coupons. So if you purchase 100 nail polishes at $1 each and then use 100 coupons and throw in some ExtraBuck coupons or rewards that help towards that tax (which would be $6 here in Maryland), you would earn $10 in Beauty Club rewards. Just like that. Yeah, I did it and no, I don't paint my nails. I donated them all. I got paid $10 to carry out $100 in products.

Remember the beauty club resets at the end of the calendar year, so if you are $2 away from your next rewards on December 31st, I suggest you find a way to spend that $2.

In addition to the $5 for every $50 spent, the beauty club also gives you a $3 reward on your birthday. I guess they want you to look beautiful at least one day out of the year.

Remember, you have to sign up for the beauty club, you can ask your cashier how or you can do it online or on the CVS App. It is not automatic.

Note there is also a Diabetes Extra Care advantage club also for diabetics.

Register your card in the pharmacy

Fill 10 Prescriptions at CVS using your ExtraBuck card and you will receive a $5 ExtraBuck reward. This is not automatic. You must sign up and you must sign up all family members.

Sign up online and add the CVS App to your phone

You will often be able to print CVS coupons directly from their website. You can also browse the app for deals based upon the type. For instance, you can search deals that result in ExtraBuck rewards.

Quarterly ExtraBucks

CVS tracks quarterly spending on your extra care card and at the end of each quarter (April 1, July 1, October 1 and January 1) you will receive a bonus reward for your quarterly spending. While this is exciting to actually get money back from your purchases, the person with the least amount of quarterly ExtraBucks wins. Why? Because this number is based upon the actual amount of cash money that you paid out of pocket, after all coupons, after all rewards. You receive 2% back for your out of pocket expenses rounded to the nearest .50 cents increments. If you spend $50 cash out of pocket during that quarter, you will receive a $1 ExtraBuck reward at the end of the quarter. If you spend $600 you will receive a $12 ExtraBuck reward. So while that $12 looks nice you spent $600 to get there. I like my quarterly ExtraBuck rewards to be .50 cents or below!

CVS Cash Cards

Although I haven't seen them in a while, CVS will sometimes do promotions that will result in CVS cash cards instead of extra care bucks rewards. For instance, spend $30 on paper towels and get a $10 cash card. One thing that I like about CVS when you do the ExtraBuck and cash card deals, when you are close, they go ahead and give it to you. For instance, the paper towels are $9.99 each and although three of them will come to a total of $29.97, you will most likely still get the $10 cash card. You won't need to go buy another $9.99 pack. I don't believe that this is written in stone anywhere, it's just always seems to work that way. Worst case scenario, if you don't receive the reward at $29.97, CVS deals accumulate, so you can do another transaction and get above $30 to get the reward. You are able to use CVS cash cards just like cash in the CVS store. The cash cards are not linked to your particular card.

What in the world is a filler?

You will often hear people speak of a filler. Sometimes after you have used all of your manufacturer coupons and your CVS coupons and your ExtraBuck rewards, sometimes you may get into the negative. Also, sometimes you may have a $5 ExtraBuck reward but your total is only $4.75, you don't want to lose that quarter (and sometimes the cashier will NOT mark that down), find something that is a quarter to get your money's worth out of that reward. CVS does not give cash back, you will need to purchase something to make the total go above negative. Caramels at the register are my favorite. Another popular section in the store to get fillers is in the travel/trial section of the store.

Finding CVS sales

CVS sales run Sunday through Saturday. I go through the advertisements when I receive them and mark off items that I need and items that look like a good deal. I look through my extra care coupons and see if any of them can be used on the products that are on sale this week. I then search the databases (Couponcadet.com, Southernsavers.com) to see if coupons exist for the upcoming sales. If I have the coupons, I locate and cut them.

You are able to use many of the money saving rebate/cash back apps that I mentioned earlier at CVS to save even more money.

I know I've given you quite a bit of information about CVS, but remember this is one of my preferred stores because there is so much potential. They are very coupon friendly.

CHAPTER 13: GETTING THE MOST OUT OF THE DEPARTMENT STORE... (PUTTING ALL THAT YOU'VE LEARNED IN ACTION)

Prior to "extreme" couponing, I used to get all of my household, health and beauty products from Walmart. I rarely go to Walmart now unless I can find a deal.

Walmart does not double their coupons. I will not grocery shop at Walmart because it makes more sense for me to shop at my local grocery store that does double coupons and allows stacking of store coupons.

There are a few benefits of shopping at Walmart though. Walmart price matches their competitors and pays overage.

Price matching is when another store has a product on sale for less than Walmart (or any other store that price matches). All you have to do is show the advertisement to the Walmart employee and Walmart will match the competitor's price. They will even match Amazon prices (as long as they are not from third party sellers).

Per Walmart's current coupon policy, *if coupon value exceeds the price of the item, the excess may be given to the customer as cash or applied toward the basket purchase.*

While both of these policies are attractive, sometimes it is difficult to successfully accomplish either.

Once I began "extreme" couponing, I discovered Target. Prior to couponing, I rarely visited Target. By being able to stack store and manufacturer's coupons amongst other deals, you are able to save quite a bit of money at Target.

First, sign up for Target mobile coupons. Currently, to sign up, all you need to do is text COUPONS to 827438 (TARGET). Periodically, Target will text you coupons and all you need to do is show the cashier the text at the register.

In addition to mobile coupons, visit Target's website. They have internet printable Target and Manufacturer coupons.

Target also has Cartwheel. Cartwheel is a mobile app on your phone that you are able to go through and select different products to save money on. My favorite part about Cartwheel is that you are able to actually scan the product in the store and if there is a Cartwheel deal, then you are able to select that deal and when you show your Cartwheel code at the register, you are able to save money.

Target often has deals that produce Target gift cards. For instance, buy 4 bottles of body wash and get a $5 gift card. You are able to stack manufacturer coupons and store coupons to purchase the body wash and then turn around and get a gift card back. The gift card is Target cash, you can use it on your next transaction on anything in the store.

One other bonus at Target is the Target Red Card. You link your checking account to the Target Red Card and when you use the Red Card to check out, you automatically save 5% off your entire purchase. On top of everything else that you saved, 5% extra is the icing on the cake.

Target only allows four like coupons per transaction. This limits the shelf clearers from clearing the shelves when there is an amazing deal.

CHAPTER 14: COUPON LINGO

When you enter into the world of couponing, you will quickly begin to think that couponers speak another language. When you are on social media sites couponing pages, you will feel as if you are a foreign exchange student. I've compiled a list of some of the common terms that couponers use. Don't worry if you can't find something in this list that you need to know, don't forget, you can always ask Google.

Term	Meaning
AC	After Coupon
AR	After Rebate
B1G1	Buy 1 Get 1 Free
B2G1	Buy 2 Get 1 Free
BC	Before Coupon (the regular price before using any coupons)
Blinkies	Blinkies are the coupons that come from the machine attached to the store shelf that spits out coupons.
BOGO	Buy 1 Get 1 Free
BOLO	Be on the lookout (for clearance, etc.)
Cash Cards	Cash cards are distributed for completing a deal, they are used as cash at the store it was acquired from.
CATS	Catalina Coupons – the little machine at the register spits out Catalina coupons. They can be manufacturer coupons, store coupons or cash off coupons.

DND	Do Not Double – referring to DND being written on a coupon. It tells the cashier not to double the coupon, but refer back to the chapter 8 regarding doubling coupons.
EB	ExtraBuck (CVS)
ECB	Extra Care Buck (CVS)
FAC or FAR	Free after coupon or Free after rebate
Glitch	A glitch is when there is an incredible deal that is too good to be true, and most likely it is. For instance you see sneakers selling online for .01 cent each. The manufacturer didn't mean to do this. Often, glitch deals are a waste of time because the orders are usually cancelled.
Hang Tags	Coupons hanging on a product
IPs	Internet Printables
ISO or IDSO	In search of or In Desperate search of – used by couponers when they are in search of a specific deal on a product or a coupon.
IVC	Instant Value Coupons are store coupons distributed by Walgreens in their monthly coupon book found in store or online.
Marking down a coupon	It is at the store's discretion to mark a coupon down. They may choose to do so if the coupon is going to give you overage (the coupon is worth more than the cost of the product). Say you have a $1 coupon and the product is only .75 cents. The store can give you the full value of the coupon and it would result in .25 cents overage or they can decide to mark the coupon down to .75 cents. If a store marks your coupon down, they are supposed to write on the coupon .75 cents, otherwise they will still be collecting $1 from the manufacturer which is unethical.
Matchups	When you study the store's sales and match the sales up with available coupons.
MM	Moneymaker - A deal that results in overage, it "makes the couponer money".
MF	Manufacturer
MQ	Manufacturer Coupon

NLA	No Longer Available – usually referred to a coupon that was once distributed but not available anymore. For instance, an internet printable once available is no longer printing.
OOP	Out of Pocket – referred to as the final amount of money that was spent out of pocket after all deals and coupons have been used.
OOS	Out of Stock
Overage	Sometimes, when you stack coupons with store sales you end up in the having more coupons than the product actually costs. Overage depends on the store's coupon policy. Some stores will give overage money back to you in cash, some require that you use it in store (on another product) and not receive cash back and some stores do not allow it at all and will mark down a coupon. Overage is the same thing as a moneymaker.
OYNO	On Your Next Order – the Catalina that prints out at the register for a dollar amount after purchasing a specific product is good to use "On Your Next Order".
Q	Coupon
Peelies	Coupons attached to products – that you have to peel off.
PG	P&G Insert
Raincheck	When a store has a sale and the product is no longer in stock, you should be able to obtain a raincheck from customer service. The raincheck allows you to come back at a later date after the sale is over and purchase the product at the sale price.
Red Box	The coupon machine/Price Checker at CVS
RP	Red Plum Insert
RR	Register Rewards – Cash coupons distributed at Walgreens
Run Deal	A run deal is when a store has a great deal (clearance, mark down, etc.) and you need to run because quantities are limited and the deal may end at any time.
Shelf Clearer	The individual that hears of a deal and rushes to the store and purchases every single one of the products

	in the store (and clears the shelf) without any regard for other shoppers.
SS	Smart Source coupon insert
TP	Tearpad – a pad of coupons usually found near a product
UPC	Universal Product Code – the barcode on a product
Ups	Up rewards distributed at Rite Aid
YMMV	Your Mileage May Vary – your success of doing this deal may vary at another store. This term is often overused. Any legitimate coupon deal should be able to be repeated at any other store as long as you have that store and the coupons. Clearance and some prices vary from store to store and that is when YMMV should come into play.

CHAPTER 15: COUPONER'S PROBLEMS

Once you get out there and start couponing, you will quickly learn that some stores despise couponers. Don't take it personally, I never have.

I've learned that many of the stores have been jaded by couponers. Some "couponers" fraudulently misuse coupons. They try to use expired coupons, they try to use coupons on the wrong products or the wrong sizes and they copy internet printable coupons (of which the store doesn't get paid). They abuse the coupon policies. They argue with the cashiers and argue with the managers when they are wrong and when they don't get their way, they have the audacity to call corporate and complain.

Don't get me wrong, if you have a bad experience in a store, by all means, call corporate and get them involved. They need to know what is going on in their stores because they are responsible for their employees. But, don't you dare call corporate when you are dead wrong and they did not give into your demands.

Couponers hold up lines when their coupons aren't organized. I will stand back in the store and make sure that all of my coupons are straight and in order before proceeding to the register. When I see that there is a line and I have a lot of coupons, I will allow other customers to go in front of me. Yes, I am a customer too, but remember, you get more bees with honey. I can buy a cart full of stuff and use a stack of coupons while a line forms behind me, I have the right, I am a paying customer too, however, when I leave and the customers behind me give the cashier grief because I held up his line, the next time I come in, he is going to despise me.

So, I recommend, prior to walking to the register, confirm that you have the correct coupons for the correct products and have all of your coupons in order (I turn them all the same way for easy scanning by the cashier). Sometimes coupons do beep, it happens, but if you have the correct product then you should be fine. However, some stores will not accept the coupon at all if it beeps. Remember, it is their prerogative.

If you work to be an educated and legitimate couponer, you will soon be separate from the rest.

Sometimes, you will be faced with having to return a defective product that you purchased with a coupon. Generally, if you just purchased the product, the store should be able to return any cash that you paid out of pocket and return the coupon to you. If the coupon is not available, the store should refund the coupon value to you either by cash or in store credit. It is up to the manager to make that decision, however, remember (and you should remind him/her) that the store will be reimbursed for that coupon if it is submitted to the manufacturer.

Sometimes, it is just an argument that I do not want to have. If I need the product, I will exchange it for a non-defective replacement. If I can live without the product, and I didn't spend any of my cash out of pocket on the product, I will throw it in the trash and move on with my life.

Another thing that you must do is watch the register and double check your receipts to confirm that the products are ringing up at their advertised price. I have one store that I shop at regularly where I am always overcharged. I am beginning to think that they do it on purpose to catch the folks that don't pay attention.

Depending on the store, (check your store's policy) sometimes, if the register rings up wrong, you are entitled to keep that product and get your money back.

CHAPTER 16: THE COUPONER'S LIFESTYLE

Once you begin to save money on groceries, toiletries and household items, eventually you will become spoiled. You will soon try to save money in every area of your life.

You'd be surprised at how many corners that you can cut just by trying. I'm going to share a few of my experiences.

Renting a car: I had to rent a car for the weekend. I went online to a popular car rental place and searched for a car and the rate. I put in that I would pick it up at the location closest to my house. I then put in a location that is just three more miles down the road and the price dropped dramatically. I played around with the website and it appears that the car rental place has you paying for convenience. I put in my home address as a different location (closer to the second location) and the results were opposite. The car rental location further from my fake-address (which was actually closer to my real address) was now less expensive. So when you are searching for rates on rental cars, don't be afraid to go a few extra miles down the road to save a couple dollars.

Price Comparison: Just like with the rental car, I've discovered that it doesn't hurt to shop around on other things that I used to just pay the asking price because I didn't think that it would be cheaper anywhere else.

For instance, I needed a part for my refrigerator so I called several different companies looking for this part and compared prices. I was quoted $20 to $180 for the exact same part. The exact same part. Do you hear me? There was a price difference of $160 for the exact same part (same manufacturer, brand new and not rebuilt). The first company that I called told me $180. In the past, I would have gave them $180 because I initially thought that the part was supposed to be expensive.

We've become accustomed to shopping around on the internet, but we can't be complacent when it comes to shopping locally.

Cellphone service: Everyone will give you advice on a cellphone provider, from my experience the one that incorporates everything and doesn't nickel and dime you on data, etc. is the one that works for me. Don't be afraid to enter into a contract to save a few dollars. Why? Because, right now, many cellular companies are more than willing to buy you out of your contract to switch to them. Don't be afraid to patronize those companies that have no contracts. They really are what they say they are and they really do what they say they do.

Cable and Internet Providers: I recently called my phone company (who also is my cable company) and complained about the bill. I told them that it was just entirely too much and we needed to review it. Just like that, I saved $40 per month. They said that I didn't have a contract and if I agreed to a two year contract, it would go down $40 per month. I have no plans whatsoever to switch to the other local provider, so why not? The young lady told me to call back as soon as I get notice (in two years) that it is going up and re-do the contract. I've paid three bills since it has gone down $40 per month and it really has gone down $40 per month. I saved almost $1000 just by asking. ($40 times 24 months).

Car Insurance: Who knows anything about car insurance? The average consumer doesn't know what they are paying for on their policy, they just hope that they have coverage when they have an accident. When was the last time that you called your insurance agent and asked them to review your policy? You may be paying for coverage that you may not need.

For instance, do you have more than one vehicle? Are you paying for rental car coverage? Why would you pay for rental car coverage (it's not cheap) if you have a back-up vehicle? That is one corner to cut.

Are you paying for full coverage on an older car? If you have a car loan from a bank, you are required to carry full coverage, but if you don't and the car isn't worth much, you may be wasting your money. Search online and find the value of your car. Look on your policy and see your comprehensive (fire, theft and vandalism) deductible and your collision (at fault accident) deductible and note the premium that you are paying. (Remember if your insurance policy is a six-month policy, multiply the premium times two).

If your yearly premium plus your deductible is more than or close to the value of your car, you need to take full coverage off that vehicle. You are paying too much money.

The reason why you are paying too much money is because you will pay the yearly premium whether you have an accident or not, but let's just assume that you have an accident. You will have paid the yearly premium, plus you will have to pay the insurance deductible, when you add these two numbers together and it is more than the actual value of your car, you are wasting your money. If these numbers are close, it's up to you. You will take a loss if you don't have an accident (by gambling and paying your yearly insurance premium), but you will come out on top if you do have an accident (until they raise your rates for having an accident).

I'll put it in a chart for you:

Yearly Insurance Premium	PLUS	Collision Ded	Total	Is it greater than or less than?	Veh Value	Should you have full coverage?
$1000	+	$500	$1500	>	$1200	NO
$600	+	$250	$850	<	$1200	It's up to you
$1000	+	$500	$1500	<	$5000	Yes

This is something that you will want to talk to your insurance agent about. I've heard people say that they don't want to take a loss if they have an accident, understand this, the insurance company is only obligated to pay the actual cash value of your car if it is totaled, so regardless, you will take a loss if your vehicle is not worth anything. I understand that the car is worth a million dollars to you if it is paid for and running, but it is only worth the actual cash value to the insurance company.

Also, it makes more sense to call and talk to your insurance company and ask for a review of your policy rather than jumping around from carrier to carrier to save .75 cents. You save more money by doing a review of your policy and making sure you aren't overinsured rather than going to a new company and getting bamboozled into a new policy with an introductory rate or with less coverage than you previously had.

Check with your insurance company, some companies are offering discounts for paperless policies, electronic funds transfer (taking your monthly payment directly from your bank account), paying your policy is full and good driver discounts by plugging a chip in your car to monitor your driving patterns. Call your insurance company and ask if there are any programs that you are eligible for to save some money.

Roadside Assistance: Again, I'm not going to drop any names, but there are a few roadside assistance companies out there that charge well over $100 per year to have roadside assistance. Did you know that many insurance companies offer the same exact coverage AND contract with the same exact tow truck companies that the big name car clubs use for a fraction of the price? Call your insurance company and ask them. If you have roadside assistance with your insurance company AND the big name company, you do not need both. Pick one or the other.

Insurance again: Now let's talk about your house. It only makes sense to have your home insured with the same company that you have your car insured with because many companies offer multi-line discounts. That means if you have your home and auto insurance with the same company, sometimes you can save quite a bit of money. Some companies even offer a multi-line discount if you have life insurance too. Don't forget though, if you are getting a quote to switch over one of the policies to the other company, make sure that they are giving you the exact same coverage that you already have on the old policy (or better) and that it isn't an introductory rate. Many companies can give you a cheaper rate with less coverage, so make sure they are matching your coverage.

Shopping online: There are so many choices when shopping online which is how we are able to save so much money. First of all, when I shop online, I start at a **rebate** site. I always start at Ebates.com first. I'm sure there are other websites that people use to get rebates, but Ebates has always worked best for me. Anytime that I shop online, I go to Ebates.com and see if the store that I plan to shop at is in their system. I click on that store through their site. When I do this, I am automatically registered to get cash back from whatever purchases that I make at the site that I am shopping from. For instance, it will say, earn 3% for shopping at XXX.com site. So if I spend $100 at XXX.com site, then I will get 3% back from that purchase. It's not a million dollars, but every penny counts. I have received over $1000 from Ebates in the past few years.

Also, if I plan to purchase something at a local retailer, I check to see if that retailer is on Ebates.com. I then shop online and choose pick up in store. When I do this, I am still able to get cash back.

Another thing I do when I am shopping online is I search for **coupon codes**. Ebates.com often has codes available on their site for use, but usually I will just google (Name of Store) coupon code. I am fortunate to find codes for free shipping, $25 off $100 purchase, 25% off purchase, etc.

In fact, I try to find coupon codes for everything including the movies, car rental, clothes, shoes, makeup, etc.

Customer reward programs: Many restaurants and stores offer customer reward programs. You may need to download their app or inquire in store. Many restaurants offer buy 9 meals and the 10th meal is free deals. I never walk into a restaurant without looking on their website and see if they have a customer rewards program, an app and/or coupons. Definitely, don't sleep on the birthday clubs. I sign up at every restaurant in my area that offers discounts and free food for your birthday. I am able to celebrate my birthday the entire month of June! Usually, it is just as simple as providing them with your birthday when you sign up for their rewards programs.

My car: I told you I save money everywhere. I am loyal to Toyotas and I am on my fourth Camry. It's just the style and quality of car that I love. I'm not telling you to run out and buy a Camry, but I'm going to tell you how I save money with my Camry. I have a Toyota Camry Hybrid. I paid slightly more for this car than if I had bought the regular Toyota Camry, but the little bit of money that I paid extra has more than paid me back over the period of time that I have owned it. It costs the same amount of money to fill up my current hybrid Camry vs. my last regular Camry, the tank sizes are the same. However, my last Camry only got 300 miles to a tank of gas, while my hybrid Camry gets 500 miles to a tank of gas. Every time that I go to the gas station and fill up for the same amount of money, I get an extra half of a tank of gas. If it costs me $40 to fill up from empty and I am getting an extra 200 miles out of that gas, I am getting $20 worth of free gas each time that I fill up.

Also, because my engine shifts back and forth between electric and the regular engine, I am able to save on maintenance. Manufacturers recommend that you get your oil changed every 3,000 miles on regular cars, I am able to get my oil changed every 5,000 on my hybrid car.

So, I'm not telling you to run out and buy a hybrid Camry (because I don't want everyone having the same car as me), but I am saying when you purchase any vehicle, figure out what that vehicle is going to cost you over the long run. You may save a couple dollars purchasing a different car but is all the money that you save going to be poured into the gas tank?

Speaking of cars: Keeping up the maintenance on your car saves you in the long run. I agree, it can get pretty expensive, but in the long run, it is cheaper than having to buy a new car.

I faithfully get my oil changed according to the manufacturer's recommendation. If I didn't want to get dirty, I'd change my oil myself. Instead, I do the next best thing. When it's time for an oil change, I search for coupons and take the car to the best deal that I can find (of course I'm referring to reputable establishments). The dealership is always so much more expensive, I try to patronize the small businesses instead.

I recently needed to change the air filters in my car (I have two), so I called the dealership to inquire on price. I was astounded at the price so I decided to look up how to do replace these air filters myself. I watched a video and went to the local automotive store and purchased the filters for 75% less than what the dealership quoted me and I was able to change these filters in five minutes. So while I refuse to change my own oil, there are many things that I am quite capable of doing myself for a fraction of the cost.

How do you save money?   Visit me on Facebook at www.facebook.com/authorkadenmatthews and let me know.

CHAPTER 17: WELCOME TO THE WONDERFUL WORLD OF COUPONING

It doesn't matter why you have decided that you want or need to coupon, it only matters that you have made a conscientious decision to save money. You could be a single parent struggling to make ends meet or a wealthy businessperson who would like to keep their wealth, either way around, it's your money and you should stretch it as far as it can possibly go.

To recap everything that I said:
1. Find coupons: they are everywhere and once you find them, hold on to them until they expire, hopefully a deal will come.
2. Organize your coupons: figure out the system that works best for you.
3. Study coupon policies: go to the websites of the stores that you shop at and print the policies or ask for a copy of the coupon policy at the customer service desk.
4. Build a deal: read circular flyers and be willing to go to different stores to get the best deal, use manufacturer and store coupons, look for coupons in databases, rebate/cash back apps, Catalina deals and don't forget your store loyalty cards.

5. Build new habits: change your thinking, usually the smallest package is best when it comes to saving money using coupons.
6. Start at the store you've been shopping at.
7. Take everything that you've learned and put it in action: there's nothing to it but to do it!
8. Now GO!

I wrote this book from my heart. So many people are struggling just to make ends meet. So many people ask me to shop for them, but not only do I not have time, but I am not doing anything for them by shopping for them. *Give a man a fish and you feed him for the day; teach a man to fish and you feed him for a lifetime -* Chinese Proverb.

Give a man a coupon, or a bottle of body wash and he will smell good for a day, teach him to coupon and he will smell good for a lifetime. - Me.

If I help just one person adjust their thinking and save a few dollars, then I have accomplished what I set out to do.

If I have helped you save any of your hard earned money, please let me know. Please go to Amazon and post a review and let me know how I helped you.

Please visit me on my website at www.KadenMatthews.com or Instagram @kadenmatthewsworld or on Facebook at www.facebook.com/authorkadenmatthews.

Please share this book with a friend.

INDEX

ACKNOWLEDGMENTS

I would like to take this time to acknowledge my coupon team --
they help me to be an amazing couponer. You can't do it all by
yourself, so build your own coupon team and make it work!

I would like to thank the many amazing coupon groups on
Facebook and the #couponcommunity on Instagram.

ABOUT THE AUTHOR

Washington, D.C. area native author Kaden Matthews has been
extreme couponing for several years. She has taught family, friends
and strangers the art of saving money.
She is married with three children, three dogs and a cat that she
feeds quite well, thanks to coupons.
She enjoys reading, writing fiction and non-fiction books and what
else? Shopping.

Made in the USA
Lexington, KY
02 August 2018